Ripped from the Headlines

The Environment

Population

by Gail B. Stewart

ERICKSON PRESS

Yankton, South Dakota

ERICKSON PRESS

LIBRARY OF CONGRESS CATALOGING-IN-PUBLICATION DATA

Stewart, Gail B. (Gail Barbara), 1949–
  Ripped from the headlines : population / by Gail B. Stewart.
     p. cm.
  Includes bibliographical references and index.
  Summary: This high-interest book for low-reading-level students examines the effects of global population growth. Topics discussed include: worldwide population growth, population distribution, the effects of disease and the development of modern medicine, strain on the earth's resources, and solutions for minimizing the effects of overpopulation.
  ISBN 978-1-60217-026-1 (hardcover : alk. paper)
1. Population—Juvenile literature. 2. Population—Environmental aspects—Juvenile literature. I. Title.
  HB883.S744 2008
  304.6—dc22
                                                                          2007045778

Printed in the United States of America

Contents

The Ticking Clock

In a small room in the U.S. Census Bureau is a special sort of clock. It is called World POPClock. "POP" is short for "population." But it does not tell time. Instead, it shows the number of people on the planet. Large computers work nonstop. They gather data from countries around the world.

The computers keep track of births. They also keep track of deaths. Then a large computer crunches the numbers. This tells experts about how many people live in each country. It tells them how many people live in the world today. It also gives them an idea of how many people will live on the planet years from now.

October 12, 1999, was a special day for the POPClock. On that day, the world's population rose to 6 billion. Never before had there been so many people living at one time on earth.

Crowded Places, Empty Spaces

Eight years later the world's population had grown even more. In September 2007 it reached 6.5 billion. Experts say that by 2050 the number will be 10 billion. This is very fast growth. Some people see no problem with the growing numbers. Others worry that the earth will become too crowded.

A crowded street in Shanghai, China, bustles with activity.

Newborn babies in India are welcomed into the world.

Some places are already very crowded. China is a very large country. It also has a very large population. More people live in China than in any other country. More than 1.3 billion people live in China. India is another large country. It has the next largest population. More than 1.1 billion people live in India.

Other places are not crowded at all. Greenland is the largest island in the world. But fewer than 60,000 people live there. Mongolia, in central Asia, is another large country. For its size, its population is small. Only 2.9 million people live there.

Why Population Matters

Numbers like these interest population experts. Population experts are called demographers. Demographers use these and other numbers for many purposes.

They look at how many people live in a place. They also look at whether that population has what it needs to live. People need more than space. They need clean water. They need food. They need energy to keep their homes warm. They need schools and roads and hospitals, too.

Demographers study populations and the things they need to live. Sometimes a population in one place does not have what it needs. There may not be enough fresh water. Maybe there is not enough energy to heat homes. There may not be enough land to grow food. In cases like these, the population may be too big.

Today many experts are concerned about population. They worry that too many people do not have the things people need to live. They also worry about the strain people put on the earth. People are not always careful about how they treat the planet's water and air. Sara Gilbert is a science teacher in New York. She says people are not separate from the rest of the earth.

"We are part of the environment," she says. "It's a vast system. If the earth is not healthy, we won't be healthy, either. Sometimes people forget this. They act as though the planet is here just to be used. But it is a give and take. From the smallest insect to the most powerful kings and presidents. If one part of the system is sick, the rest are affected, too. All of life on earth is connected." [1]

The U.S. population is at 300 million and growing according to this display.

Growing by the Minute

The number on the World POPClock grows bigger each second. No one can say for sure if this is cause for alarm. They do not know if there are enough of the things people need. They do not know for sure if there will be a time when the earth has too many people. They do not know because there have never been as many people on the earth as there are now.

The experts disagree on many things. Some worry about the future. They think the rising numbers spell big problems. Others believe there is plenty of room for more people. Any problems that arise, they say, can be solved.

The subject of population is an important one. There are smart people on both sides of the question. But there is one thing on which they do agree. The earth's population is growing faster than ever before. And no one can say for certain what that will mean.

Chapter 1

More than Just a Number

Earth's population is always changing. But usually it does not change a lot. Every year nearly 128 million babies are born. And every year about 59 million people die. But once in a while there is a big change.

In 1918 there was a big change. It was caused by a pandemic. A pandemic is a disease that spreads throughout the world. It was a very deadly kind of flu. It killed between 50 million and 80 million people. World population fell that year more than most years.

This was not the first time a disease killed millions of people. There have been other pandemics. And they have affected world population much like this one did. One pandemic took place in A.D. 500. It was especially deadly. It was a fever that killed very quickly. Experts say that world population at the time was about 150 million. They think that the disease killed 100 million people. That was two-thirds of the people on earth at the time.

No Easy Answer

Experts understand changes like these. They know that pandemics can cause big drops in population. But they have seen something new in the last 150 to 200 years. During this time earth's population has grown faster than ever before. And it continues to grow.

A victim of an Indonesian flu pandemic is laid to rest in 2005.

Some people wonder if it is growing too much or too fast. About 6.5 billion people on the planet is a lot of people. But is it too many people? This seems like a simple question. But it does not have a simple answer.

Looking Back

One way experts try to answer the question is by looking at history. They study how and why pop-

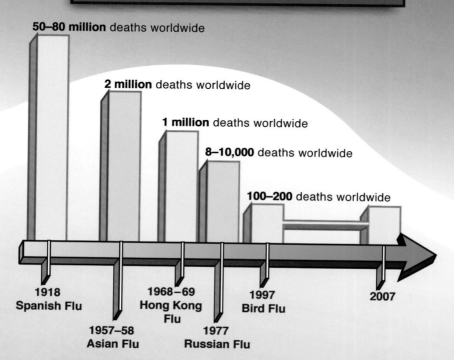

Significant Dates in Pandemic History

As this pandemic timeline shows, the devastating effects of pandemics have decreased due to advances in modern medicine.

50–80 million deaths worldwide

2 million deaths worldwide

1 million deaths worldwide

8–10,000 deaths worldwide

100–200 deaths worldwide

1918
Spanish Flu

1957–58
Asian Flu

1968–69
Hong Kong
Flu

1977
Russian Flu

1997
Bird Flu

2007

Source: www.news.cornell.edu

Dying Little Towns

There are places in the United States where population is falling. Many small towns are disappearing. In little towns in Nebraska and Iowa, young people are leaving. They do not want to be farmers like their parents. They are moving to cities, where there is more to do. As a result the little farm towns are dying.

Orchard is a little town in central Iowa. Years ago it was a busy place. There were lots of young families. Now the average age in Orchard is 75. The young families have moved away. Jim Lack is the mayor of Orchard. "We had banks and grocery stores . . . just like any other town," he says. But in the past 30 years Orchard has shrunk. The young families have moved away. People cannot buy gas there. They cannot even buy a gallon of milk. Says Lack, "There are no businesses here at all."

Quoted in O.K. Henderson, "Governor Vilsack Visits Orchard in Walking Tour," Radio Iowa, September 28, 2005. www.radioiowa.com/gestalt/go.cfm?objectid=78D046D6-B54F-4C8F-BCE8F2844E573365.

ulations change over time. They try to apply what they learn to today's population concerns.

Experts know that humans have been on the earth for at least 100,000 years. For many thousands of years, the population stayed small. The number of new births was high. But the number of deaths was also high. Many children died when they were very young. They did not grow up to have children of their own. So the population grew slowly.

Over the centuries things changed. Humans learned to farm. They did not need to live by hunting wild animals. They raised cows or goats or pigs. They grew crops. They saved any extra food for lean times. That way they had a constant food supply. That made them healthier, and they lived longer.

The population grew a little faster. Then around 1850 something changed. About this time the number of people on earth began to grow more quickly. And it has climbed higher and higher ever since then.

Living Longer

The reason for the increase was not more newborn babies. Many parents in 1850 had the same number of babies as their parents and grandparents did. It was the number of deaths that changed. Before the mid-1800s many diseases killed people. People also died from sore throats and infections. Many women died giving birth. There were no drugs to treat illnesses or infections. There were no hospitals. If a person got sick, he or she usually died.

After the mid-1800s the death rate in Europe and North America went way down. That is because people were healthier. They were healthier because of new inventions for doctors. The thermometer let doctors keep track of fevers. The stethoscope let

Global Population Distribution

Despite being two of the largest countries in the world, China and India are still two of the most crowded with populations of over 1 billion.

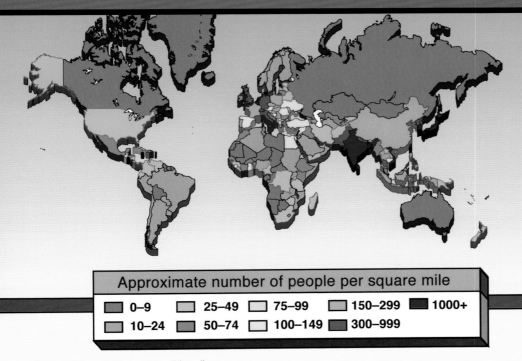

Approximate number of people per square mile

0–9	25–49	75–99	150–299	1000+
10–24	50–74	100–149	300–999	

Source: www.wikimedia.org

them listen to the heart and lungs. By this time scientists had also discovered germs. They realized that germs could make people sick. They came up with ways to keep that from happening.

The death rate fell for other reasons, too. People lived longer because they had better food. They learned about the health benefits of fresh fruits and vegetables. And better roads helped get those foods to hungry people.

People today live longer lives thanks to modern medicine.

These improvements made a real difference. People began living longer than in years past. In the 1400s most people did not live past age 36. By the mid-1800s most lived into their 60s. This change in how long people lived allowed the population to grow.

Growing and Shrinking

Experts say that world population is rising quickly. They think it will rise faster in the next decades than ever before. But they cannot be sure. Populations are growing in some places. But they are shrinking in other places.

Disease is shrinking populations in parts of Africa. There many adults are dying of AIDS. In some villages almost no healthy adults are left. Children are raising themselves. This can be seen in Swaziland, a small country in southern Africa. In 2007 its population was 1.1 million. But more than 40 percent of the people between 15 and 49 had AIDS. And most of those were dying.

Nowhere on earth is life as short as in Swaziland. Sacin Desai is a doctor there. He works in an AIDS clinic. He feels that he is doing good work. But it

AIDS is shrinking populations in parts of Africa.

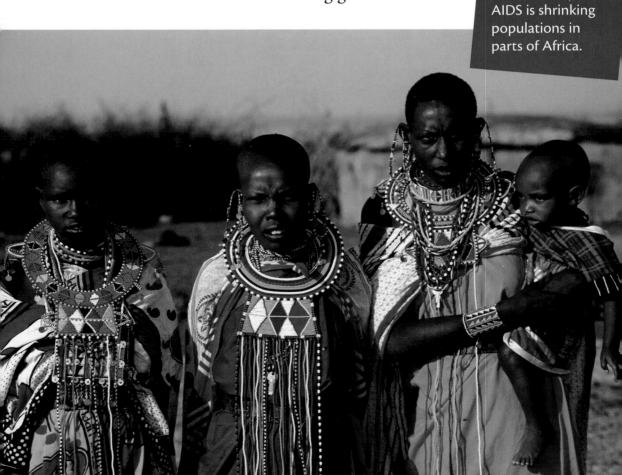

is not enough. For every patient he treats, ten cannot even get to his clinic. That makes him sad and frustrated. He says, "That's the thing that keeps going into my head."[2] David McCollum agrees. He works with AIDS patients, too. He says AIDS is affecting modern people like no other disease before it. He calls it "the disaster of our time."[3]

Too Many or Not?

So some populations are growing and some are shrinking. What does this mean for the future? Experts are divided. Some say that sooner or later,

A doctor works with a young patient in a South African AIDS clinic.

Hunger destroys lives. Some think hunger will worsen as world population grows.

the planet will be too crowded. There will not be enough room for everyone to live. They say there will not be enough room to grow all the food for those people. There will not be enough water. The shortages of food and water will cause hunger and disease.

Art Hobson teaches science at the University of Arkansas. He thinks that the world is already too crowded. He thinks that problems like these lie ahead.

He says, "This planet is just packed—however you look at it."[4]

But other experts do not agree. They know that the planet has limited resources. But they think people can find ways to use those resources more wisely. And then there will be enough for all the world's people.

Population is more than just a number. It is also important to look at whether people have what they need to live. Is there enough food and water? Do people have clean air to breathe? The answers to these questions can help answer the big question: "How many is too many people?"

Chapter 2

Population and the Environment

The most important need for the world's population is the planet itself. The earth is the source of air, land, and water. It has millions of types of plants and animals. When the planet is healthy, all of these living things can thrive. But as earth's human population grows, people make greater demands on the environment. And those demands can put a strain on resources such as air, land, water, and wildlife.

Needing Space

More people means a greater need for houses. Building new houses requires land. Trees are often cut down to provide more land for new houses. More houses also mean more businesses where people can buy the things they need. More land is needed for these businesses. More trees must be cut down.

Some forests have been destroyed to make room for new houses and businesses. This has happened in California. There, redwood trees have been cut

The earth's resources make life possible for plants, animals, and people.

down to make room for new homes and business-es. "This is so sad," says Eileen Stevens, a forestry student. She lives in Modesto, California. "These coastal redwoods are amazing trees. They can live more than 2,000 years. They are the tallest living things on the planet. I've seen firsthand how beautiful they are. But so many are being cut down, either for their wood or to make room for homes."

Stevens says it is too bad when any trees are destroyed. "But these trees are special," she says. "We as a population haven't been good for the redwoods. We aren't always making wise choices. We need to learn to live in tune with our environment. Too many times we try to conquer it, instead."[5]

Forests worldwide have been cut down to make room for new houses.

Better Choices

People around the world are making changes. They know that populations will grow. But they have tried to find ways to protect resources. They have tried to use resources wisely. In some places, people have created "green" neighborhoods. In these neighborhoods, people try to use fewer natural resources. In some cases, homes are built with recycled materials. That way, no new material is needed. Sometimes solar panels store heat from the sun. This is a way to heat homes using less energy. These ideas can help save resources.

A sign marks a corn crop being grown for use in biofuels.

A Threat to the Inuit Population

Sometimes pollution can threaten an entire population. The Inuit population in northern Canada is in trouble. Their air is polluted. The water around them is polluted, too. It is full of dangerous chemicals. This is not caused by the Inuit. They have no factories. There is no industry there. The pollution is being swept north from the United States.

The Inuit people eat meat from whales and seals. That has been their diet for generations. But the whales and seals have poisons, too. The poison is in the meat. And when people eat it, they become sick. Some suggest the Inuit eat other things, instead.

But the Inuits say no. They say they are living as Inuits have always lived. One woman says, "I am very connected to my country food. It's what sustains me." If the Inuits did not eat their traditional food, their culture would change.

Quoted in K.L. Capozza, "Inuit Life Threatened by U.S." Mindfully.org, June 11, 2001. www.mindfully.org/Air/US-Threatens-Inuit.htm.

In some city neighborhoods, people have set up community gardens. People can grow their own vegetables. They use little space. And they use little water, mostly from rain.

"Even in the city, we can do that," says Mazie Newman. She lives in a neighborhood near the Mississippi River, in Minneapolis. "I've got tomatoes and peppers growing up on my roof. You just don't need a lot of space. We reuse rainwater, so we don't waste. And it's nice to have homegrown food to share with neighbors."[6]

Dirty Air

Population growth can also affect the air. People need clean air to breathe. But many crowded cities do not have clean air.

Sometimes the problem is factories. Factories provide jobs. They also make things people need. But factories can pollute the air. This is a problem. But there is an even bigger problem.

The biggest air polluter in crowded cities is cars. As populations have increased, so have the numbers of cars. In 2006 there were about 620 million cars in the world. About 220 million of those were in the United States. This is almost one-third of all the cars on the planet.

Polluted air is harmful to people. Sometimes dirty air in a crowded place looks hazy, like a cloud. The haze is really millions of tiny particles. These are poisons left over from burned gasoline. The tiny particles are dangerous. They make it hard to breathe. Doctors warn people not to exercise on days when the air pollution is bad. They would not be able to get the oxygen their bodies need.

Many crowded cities suffer from bad air. Los Angeles, Mexico City, and Tokyo all have very large populations. All three cities also have polluted air. The worst air pollution is in Beijing in China. That city has more than 2.7 million cars. And every day, 1,000 new drivers take to Beijing's roads.

"Thick Yellow Soup"

Paul Phillips is a photographer. He traveled to China in September 2007. He took pictures at the Women's World Cup soccer games. Phillips was amazed at the pollution. It was everywhere. It blocked out the sun. "It was like thick yellow soup," he says. "I'd be standing on one end of the soccer

Factories provide needed jobs but also pollute the air.

field. And I couldn't even see the other end! I worried about all of the athletes. That kind of air isn't healthy to breathe."[7]

China's government knows the problem is serious. More than 667,000 Chinese people each year die from breathing problems caused by pollution. The government wants its people to be healthy. But making changes can be hard. And it can cost a lot of money. So, few changes are being made. And air pollution in China gets worse and worse.

Wang Finnan is a noted Chinese pollution expert. He says it is very sad. China's economic success is causing the population to become sick. "It is a very awkward situation for the country,"[8] he says.

Dirty air forces some people to wear masks as they ride to work in China.

"I Couldn't See to Drive"

Some big cities have made changes. They have tried to cut down on air pollution. Los Angeles is one city that has made changes. This city grew quickly starting in the 1940s. Millions of people came to California. They liked the idea of sunshine, warm weather, and lots of jobs. But the more people who came, the dirtier the air became.

Scientists discovered the cause. It was a mix of factory smoke, car exhaust, and sunshine. That mix created a smoky type of fog known as smog.

One woman recalls driving to work in the 1950s. The smog was so strong it hurt her eyes. "I'd have to pull over by the side of the road," she says. "My eyes were tearing so badly, I couldn't see to drive."[9]

California officials began making changes in the 1960s. They hoped these changes would lead to cleaner air. They put limits on factories. They also put limits on cars. Cars had to use a device that cut the pollution coming out of tailpipes. Little by little, the air improved. "It's not perfect," says Maryanne Lewis. She has lived in Los Angeles since 1952. "But we've got lots more sunny days than we used to."[10]

Animals in Trouble

As earth's human population grows, animals are affected, too. When land is cleared for houses and roads, animals suffer. Loss of forests and underbrush destroys habitat. The animals have no place

Prairie Potholes

Sometimes decisions about resources and population are very difficult. One decision is about prairie potholes. These are small, shallow wetlands. From the air they look like little lakes. They are found throughout Canada and the upper midwestern United States.

Wildlife depend on the potholes. They are a habitat for more than 200 species of birds. They provide food for baby birds that hatch in the spring. Potholes also prevent floods. They hold water until it seeps back into the ground.

But some farmers are draining the potholes. They say land is expensive. They want to use that land for crops. After all, the population is growing. They need to supply more and more food to the nation. This worries wildlife experts. They understand the needs of the farmers. But animal habitat is important, too. No one knows what will happen to the prairie potholes.

to build homes. They have no safe place to raise their young. After a while, species die off.

The death of one species can affect many others. Finding a balance can be hard. But it is important. David Gordon is a nature reporter. He knows about this balance. He gives the example of a box turtle eating strawberries. The strawberries help the turtle live. And the turtle helps the strawberries, too. His droppings spread the strawberry seeds. That way more plants will grow. If either were wiped out, the other would be hurt, too. Says Gordon, "Losing one species can harm many others."[11]

"That Is Very Bad News"

Scientists say some species are already dying off. In Britain bumblebees are becoming extinct. Several types of birds and 21 types of fish and turtles are, too. In the United States many birds are disappearing. There are fewer bushes and trees where they

An Indonesian zoo is now home to orangutans that once lived in a lush forest.

can nest. As a result, fewer baby birds are being born.

The balance between living things is very important. The earth has more than 100 million species of animals and plants. Scientists say hundreds of species disappear every day. "That is very bad news," says science teacher Sara Gilbert. "Once a species is gone, we can never get it back." [12]

A bluebird box provides shelter for a hungry chick.

"It Just Gives You Hope"

The growth of human populations does not mean that animals must die out. People have found ways to help wildlife. Bluebirds were common throughout the United States before the 1960s. They built their nests on wooden fence posts in fields and meadows and on farms. But tens of thousands died as more and more farmers used pesticides to protect their crops. And many more died as land was cleared to build houses for the growing population.

In the 1980s many Americans began building wooden bluebird boxes. They put the boxes out in fields or cemeteries. The boxes look like the wooden fence posts the bluebirds used to like. Now bluebirds are making a comeback. They are building nests in the boxes.

"It just gives you hope," says Marv Liepschiz. He builds bluebird boxes. "It makes you glad to help nature a little bit. Humans took over their homes. Now we can provide them with new ones." [13]

Chapter 3

Water for a Growing Population

Many things make daily life more comfortable. But there are a few things people must have to survive. One of these is water. The earth is 70 percent water. This seems like plenty of water for earth's population. But most of that water is salty. It is undrinkable. It is not good for crops, either.

About 3 percent of the earth's water is fresh. But 99 percent of that fresh water cannot be used, either. It is frozen in glaciers or Antarctic ice. Much of it is deep underground. That leaves about 1 percent of the fresh water that can be used. It is that 1 percent that must supply water for all 6.5 billion people on earth. This not as easy as it sounds.

Not Evenly Divided

Some places have lots of fresh water. Minnesota is one example. It borders Lake Superior, the world's largest lake. It has more than 15,000 other lakes, too. And it is the starting place of the Mississippi

River. The people of Minnesota do not worry about water. They have more than they need.

But other places do not have lots of fresh water. Saudi Arabia is a country in the Middle East. It is mostly desert. Saudi Arabia has no rivers. It has no lakes. The only fresh water Saudis have comes from deep underground. And it is not easy to get that water.

Sometimes, water can be shared. Places with lots of water can share with places that have too little. Colorado has lots of water. The Colorado River starts in the Rocky Mountains. It winds south all the way into Mexico. The river has more water than

The Mississippi River (shown) is one of many sources of water for the state of Minnesota.

the people in Colorado need. In 1922 Colorado agreed to share its water with six other states. They are Arizona, California, Nevada, New Mexico, Utah, and Wyoming. Those states have very little water for their populations. They depend on water from the Colorado River.

Each state is allowed a certain amount of water from the river. But sometimes it is not enough. Some states want more water from the river. Others say this would not be fair.

Limits to Sharing

Sharing water can be a problem when one population grows more than others. It is a problem for Phoenix, Arizona. Phoenix has grown very fast in

Little fresh water can be found in the dry desert landscape of Saudi Arabia.

The World's Water Availability

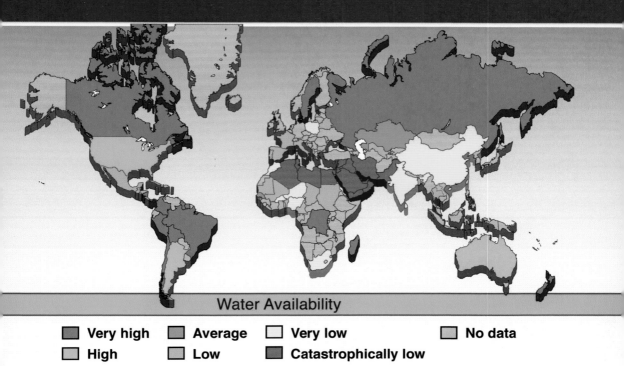

Water Availability

■ Very high ■ Average ☐ Very low ☐ No data
☐ High ☐ Low ■ Catastrophically low

Source: www.dni.gov

recent years. In 1990 it had 106,000 residents. By 2007 the number had grown to 1.6 million. With its suburbs the Phoenix area has 4 million people. One water expert says the area "continues to bust at the seams."[14]

Phoenix gets most of its water from the Colorado River. Phoenix needs a bigger share of the water. But that could create problems. Other states worry that they will get less if Phoenix gets more.

Growing Populations, Shrinking Lakes

There is another problem with water supplies. In many places they are drying up. This can be caused by overuse. It can also be caused by drought. Whatever the cause, this can be a problem for growing populations. They may lose their main water source.

This has happened in North Africa. Lake Chad is surrounded by four countries. They are Chad,

Drip Irrigation

The biggest use of water is for irrigation. In some countries, farmers use 80 percent of fresh water. They spray millions of gallons of water on crops. That way, they do not have to rely completely on rain. But irrigation is wasteful. Experts say most of the water evaporates in the sun and heat. It never gets to the roots of plants, where it could help them grow.

There is a new method for farmers. It is called drip irrigation. It uses small pipes that carry the water and nutrients directly to the roots. That way, none is lost. The sun and wind will not evaporate the water. That means less water is used on farms. And populations have more fresh water to drink.

Lake Chad provides water for millions of people but it is shrinking.

Cameroon, Niger, and Nigeria. Lake Chad was once very large. In 1990 its water supported 26 million people. By 2004 there were 37.2 million people. By 2020 experts say Lake Chad will need to support 55 million people.

But that will not happen. Lake Chad is shrinking. More and more people are using the water. They dig canals to direct the water to farmland. They take more and more water each year. As the populations grow, the water level goes down. Experts worry that the lake may one day disappear. And that would mean disaster for the population of those countries that depend on it.

Another problem area is Lake Victoria. Three nations share this lake. They are Kenya, Tanzania, and Uganda. This lake is the second largest in the world. It provides jobs as well as water. Thousands

Catching fish in Lake Victoria is becoming harder as the lake level falls.

earn money by selling the fish they catch from the lake. But little rain has fallen in this area over the last six years. Victoria has become too shallow for fishing boats. The water level has dropped 6 feet (1.8m) between 2004 and 2007. And many of the fish have died. One fisherman is worried. "If it goes like this for another five years," he says, "the lake will be empty of fish."[15]

Finding Answers

It is important to find answers to these problems. People cannot survive without clean water. One possible solution is desalination. That is a process of turning salty water into drinkable water. There are more than 12,000 desalination plants in the world. More than half are located in the Middle East, where water is scarce.

Seawater is filtered to remove sand. Tiny pieces of plant and animal life are also removed. The salty water is then pumped through a filter. This filter allows only water molecules to pass. Salt stays behind. But pumping all of that water takes lots of energy. Desalination plants use lots of coal and oil. That makes the process very dirty. Coal and oil pollute the air.

But there are new ways of removing salt from water. These new methods use cleaner kinds of energy. Some plants use solar power. Ocean waves are another promising source of energy. One water

A desalination plant in Kuwait provides needed fresh water.

expert says waves may be the best of all. They occur all day every day. He says, "It really is the next-generation technology."[16] Both waves and the sun can supply the energy needed to push salt water through the filters. It costs a lot to set up these new plants. But over time, they will make the process cheaper and cleaner.

"It's Tough, Man"

Many places on earth face water shortages. But in 2007 one little Tennessee town ran out of water. The town of Orme always got its water from a nearby spring and water-fall. But Orme has gotten very little rain. The waterfall has become only a trickle. And the spring is all but empty.

The mayor of Orme worked out a deal with an Alabama town called Bridgeport, just fifteen miles away. They let Orme tap into one of their fire hydrants to fill large containers with water. Every morning, trucks drive back and forth, carrying water to the water tank in Orme. And for three hours each night, the citizens of Orme can take showers, do laundry, and fill jugs with drinking water. Then the water tank is shut until the next day.

One resident says it is difficult living without a steady supply. "It's tough, man," he says. "Don't take your water for granted."

Quoted in Drew Jubera, "Tennessee Town Rations Water," *Atlanta Journal*, October 21, 2007, p. A1.

Wiser Use

Desalination can help. But people also need to be more careful with how they use water. In the last century the goal for experts was to find new ways to use water. But that has changed, experts say. "The next century," says one, "is going to have to be the century of efficiency."[17]

There are ways to use water more wisely. One is to recycle it. Today many cities treat wastewater to make it cleaner. Then they pipe it into oceans, rivers, or lakes. But it could be reused by farmers. They could use it to water their crops.

Another way to use water more wisely is to stop polluting it. In some places factories dump poisons into rivers and lakes. This ruins the water. It can no longer be used. In China factories have piped tons of poisons into Lake Tai. This was once thought to be one of the country's most beautiful lakes. But the poisons killed the fish. It killed the plants along the banks. It turned the water a strange shade of green. No one knows if Lake Tai can be saved. But its water can no longer be used for drinking. It cannot even be used to irrigate farmers' fields.

Water expert Peter Rogers says people take water for granted. They need to stop doing that. Otherwise, growing populations may not have the clean water they need. "It's a terrible situation around the world," Rogers says. "But it doesn't have to be."[18]

Chapter 4

Taking Action

Rising population is a fact. Some people see it as a problem. Others do not. Even so, many people have decided to act. In some cases they act alone. Other times governments or groups get involved.

Being Forceful

China is one place where the government has become involved. Since the 1970s China's leaders have been worried about population. They have been concerned that there are not enough resources to feed so many people.

At first the government urged people to have fewer children. But the population kept growing. So instead of urging, government leaders made an order. No couple could have more than one child. There were punishments for those who did not obey.

Government officials were sent to villages and towns. They reported on who was disobeying the order. Couples who were caught with more than

Young Chinese students enjoy a day in the sun.

one child were punished. Some lost their jobs. Others had to pay high fines.

The policy of one child is still in effect. But people are not happy about it. Many Chinese couples say they do not want the government to make these decisions. They say they should be the ones to decide the size of their families.

A Different Approach

In other countries people have tried other ideas. They know that a growing population can harm the air, land, and water. So they are working to slow those effects.

There are a number of ways to do that. Some places have tried to cut down on their use of coal and oil. Those fuels cause a lot of air pollution. And dirty air makes people sick. By using less coal and oil, people hope to have cleaner air.

In Great Britain scientists are testing wind energy. They have built machines that turn wind into electricity. They believe it is possible for these machines to replace oil and coal. People could heat their homes with wind energy. They could use the machines to create electricity for homes and businesses.

In the United States one company is creating power from ocean waves. Its inventors use special pumps to collect energy from waves. The clusters of pumps along the shore can turn energy into electricity. Each cluster could provide power to 750,000

A billboard reminds Chinese couples of the country's one-child policy.

一对夫妇只生育 子女

少生有利于国家,有利于家庭,有利于母亲与儿童

少生

A Little Cooperation

Pollution is a global problem. It affects populations all over the world. Sometimes nations work together to solve pollution problems. This happened on the border between Mexico and the United States. Many people in Juarez, Mexico, earn money making bricks. They earn about ten cents for every brick they make. They use special kilns, or ovens, to harden the bricks. But the kilns release lots of pollution. And the poisons drift over the border. They make the air dirty in El Paso, Texas.

Officials in El Paso wanted to clean up the air. But they understood that brick making is important to the people in Juarez. So El Paso bought new kilns for the workers. The new kilns reduce the pollution. It makes the air better on both sides of the border. One brick maker says, "It's a lot of help for all the people . . . less smoke."

Quoted in Dina Capiello, "Between a Brick and a Hard Place," *Houston Chronicle*, December 5, 2002, p. A1.

homes. Like wind energy, wave energy is clean. It will not cause pollution. This might be better than burning oil and coal for power.

Citizens Stepping Up

In the meantime, some people are slowing population's effects another way. They are working to enforce laws. Many countries already have rules for factories to follow. They can only release a certain amount of pollution. But many companies do not follow the rules. And governments sometimes do not pay attention. They do not always know who is breaking the rules.

In a Mexican town called Minatitlan, citizens are worried. There is too much pollution in their

Using fewer fossil fuels is the aim of a wind power station in Great Britain.

air. People are getting sick. Some are even dying from the polluted air. Most of the pollution comes from an oil refinery. It is releasing too much poison in the air. That is against the law. The people of Minatitlan have asked the government for help. They have complained. But they did not have proof. The government cannot accuse the refinery without proof. One man says, "Every time we go, they say, 'Show us there is a problem.'" [19]

The town is very poor. But the people care about their air. So a group of citizens took action. They

The people of Minatitlan, Mexico, are fighting pollution from a local refinery (background).

take samples of air in plastic bags. They go door to door to collect money. That pays for the sample to be tested. The citizens are hoping things will change. The government will see the proof. The refinery will have to clean itself up. And the population of Minatitlan will breathe cleaner air.

Ecotourism

Another interesting new idea changes the way people can take vacations. It is friendlier to animals. Land is not cleared for hotels and theme parks. In fact, no animal habitats are destroyed. This new idea is called ecotourism. It encourages people to visit new places. The visitors stay at small inns. Sometimes they even stay in the homes of resident hosts. But ecotourism allows people to have a close view of other populations. Visitors can see the country as it really is. Not only is ecotourism good for the planet, it also puts money in the hands of local people who need it.

One ecotourist is Barbara McCuen, from Washington. She visited Nepal, a little nation between India and China. McCuen and a small group of other visitors explored a large valley. They visited a farmer and his family. They even tried to use a cattle-driven plow. McCuen laughs as she remembers how difficult it was. "All around us were these nice straight lines," she says. "And we're plowing these crazy lines."

She says that this kind of tourism is special. It allowed her to meet a population she had never met

Pedal Power

Paris officials have been worried about air pollution in their city. Its streets are crowded with cars. That creates dirty air. Doctors say more people are having trouble breathing. In the summer of 2007 the mayor announced a new plan. Residents and visitors would be encouraged to use bikes to get around.

The plan made it easy. A network of 750 stations around the city had bikes for rent. There were 10,600 of them. For one euro (about 70 cents in the United States), anyone could rent a bike for a whole day. People had to promise to obey traffic signs. When finished, renters could drop bikes off at one of the stations.

People liked the new plan. They felt Paris was much too beautiful to drive through. Seeing it on a bike was good for the environment. And it was good for the riders, too.

before. She says, "It gives you an appreciation for how people work, how hard people's lives are." [20]

The Power of One

Some people have decided to act all by themselves. Mia is a Minneapolis sixth grader. She was reading an article for school. "It was about paper bags," she says. "It sounds boring, but it wasn't. In the United States, we use more than 11 billion bags. To make that many, they cut down 18 million trees."

Mia told her parents about what she had read. "They were amazed," she says. "Just like I was. My mom was always choosing paper at the store. Like they say, 'Paper or plastic?' She never got plastic. Everyone knows plastic is bad. So she always asked for a paper bag."

Mia and her family decided to change the way they shop. "We made cloth bags," she says. "They're big, like a shopping bag. We leave them in the car. And when we go to a store, we just use them. We

Some people have switched to bags that can be used more than once.

use them over and over. There's no pollution. And
the five of us aren't responsible for trees being
chopped down." [21]

Making a Difference

There are all kinds of ways for people to slow the
effects of a growing population. Everyone can make
a difference. There is no question that a growing population creates more challenges. More people often
means more strain on the earth. But the strain can
be reduced. The result can be a healthier planet—
one that can support all the earth's people.

Notes

Introduction: The Ticking Clock

1. Personal interview, Sara Gilbert, October 3, 2007, Minneapolis, MN.

Chapter 1: More than Just a Number

2. Quoted in Leigh Hopper, "Fight Against AIDS," *Houston Chronicle,* September 17, 2006, p. 1.
3. Quoted in Hopper, "Fight Against AIDS," p. 1.
4. Quoted in Phil Mulkins, "Overpopulation a Key Factor in Global Carbon Monoxide," *Tulsa World,* December 11, 2006, p. A19.

Chapter 2: Population and the Environment

5. Telephone interview, Eileen Stevens, November 1, 2007.
6. Personal interview, Mazie Newman, November 4, 2007, Minneapolis, MN.
7. Personal interview, Paul Phillips, October 13, 2007, Minneapolis, MN.

8. Quoted in Joseph Kahn and Jim Yardley, "As China Roars, Pollution Reaches Deadly Extreme," *New York Times*, August 26, 2007, p. 1.

9. Quoted in South Coast AQMD, "The Southland's War on Smog: Fifty Years of Progress Towards Clean Air." www.aqmd.gov/news1/Archives/History/marchcov.html.

10. Telephone interview, Maryanne Lewis, November 10, 2007.

11. David George Gordon, "Save the Planet! Five Big Problems Facing the Earth," *National Geographic Kids*, April 2003, p. 33.

12. Interview, Gilbert.

13. Personal interview, Marv Liepschiz, November 8, 2007, St. Paul, MN.

Chapter 3: Water for a Growing Population

14. Quoted in Post Carbon Cities, "Climate Change May Spur Major Population Shifts," August 1, 2007. http://postcarboncities.net/node/438.

15. Quoted in Charles Hanley, "Drought Taking Toll on Africa Lakes," *Grand Rapids Press*, January 2, 2007, p. A8.

16. Quoted in Mike Meyers, "Turning Waves into Watts," *Minnesota Star Tribune*, August 27, 2007, p. D3.

17. Quoted in Brian Skoloff, "U.S. Water Supply in Jeopardy," *Seattle Times*, October 28, 2007, p. A4.

18. Quoted in Bret Schulte, "A World of Thirst," *U.S. News & World Report*, May 27, 2007. www.usnews.com/usnews/news/articles/070527 /4hotspots.

Chapter 4: Taking Action

19. Quoted in Dina Cappiello, "Pollution in Mexico: Testing Their Own Air," *Houston Chronicle*, March 6, 2006, p. A1.
20. Quoted in Bret Schulte, "Getting Friendly with the Natives," *U.S News & World Report*, December 25, 2006, p. 80.
21. Personal interview, Mia, October 1, 2007, Minneapolis, MN.

Glossary

AIDS: A deadly disease that attacks a person's ability to fight off infection.

death rate: The number of deaths during a certain amount of time.

demographer: A person who studies population.

extinct: Gone or dead.

forestry: Having to do with trees.

green: Friendly to the environment.

pandemic: A disease that spreads throughout the world.

smog: Heavy, smoky clouds caused by sunlight and particles of air pollution.

solar: Using the sun.

stethoscope: An instrument used to listen to a patient's heart and lungs.

Bibliography

Books

Trevor Day, *Water*. New York: DK, 2007. Good information on tides, the limits of fresh water, and how water pollution occurs.

Al Gore, *An Inconvenient Truth: The Crisis of Global Warming*. New York: Viking, 2007. A good introduction to the warming that is affecting the planet. Excellent photographs and very readable text. Adapted for young readers.

Kris Hirschmann, *Pollution*. Detroit: KidHaven, 2005. Good index and a helpful section on the impact of a population's waste and garbage.

Periodicals

Charles Bremmer, "Paris Mobilizes Pedal Power to Cut Traffic and Pollution," *Times*, July 16, 2007.

H.J. Cummins, "Price of Pollution," *Minneapolis Star Tribune*, October 5, 2007.

Alex Gerber, "Population Kills," *San Diego Union-Leader*, July 7, 2005.

Charles J. Hanley, "Drought Taking Toll on Africa Lakes," *Grand Rapids Press*, January 2, 2007.

Joseph Khan, "In China, a Lake's Champion Imperils Himself," *New York Times*, October 14, 2007.

Web Sites

Darfur Information (http://darfurinformation. com/index.asp). This site contains background and current news about the crisis in Darfur. It explains the reasons for the migration of millions of people and the effect those refugees will have on population in nearby areas.

HIV and AIDS in Africa, AVERT.org (www.avert. org/aidsinafrica.htm). This site has good information on the effects of AIDS on population. It breaks down the epidemic in various nations and talks about what is being done to solve the crisis.

Kid Friendly Cities (www.kidfriendlycities.org/ 2004/articles5.html). This is a valuable Web site directed at children. It has information and breakdowns of population in twenty major American cities. The site also grades each city on the health, education, and diversity of population.

U.S. and World Population Clocks—POPClocks, U.S. Census Bureau (www.census.gov/main/ www/popclock.html). This is the site at which the World POPClock is located. It has a section explaining how the information is gathered. The site has a U.S. POPClock, too.

Index

Picture Credits

Cover Photo: © Larry Lilac/Alamy
Maury Aaseng, 12, 15, 37
SULTAN AL FAHED/Reuters/Landov, 36
AP Images, 43
AP Images/Shrabani Deb, 6
© Gary W. Carter/CORBIS, 32
JOE CHAN/Reuters/Landov, 46
© Ashley Cooper/Corbis, 24
© Natalie Fobes/CORBIS, 23
GUSTAVO GRAF/Bloomberg News/Landov, 50
© Antoine Gyori/CORBIS SYGMA, 54
© MAST IRHAM/epa/Corbis, 11
Jupiterimages Unlimited/Comstock Images, 16, 35
Jupiterimages Unlimited/Creatas Images, 53
Jupiterimages Unlimited/Goodshoot Image, 5, 22
Jupiterimages Unlimited/Photos.com, 17, 27
© Wolfgang Kaehler/CORBIS, 47
© Ed Kashi/CORBIS, 41
REINHARD KRAUSE/Reuters/Landov, 28
ANDREW PARSONS/PA Photos /Landov, 49
REUTERS/Euan Denholm/Landov, 40
REUTERS/Stephanie Hancock/Landov, 39
© David Turnley/CORBIS, 19
DARREN WHITESIDE/Reuters/Landov, 31
© Stefan Zaklin/epa/Corbis, 8
NAASHON ZALK/Bloomberg News/Landov, 18

Gail B. Stewart has written more than 240 books for children and teenagers. She lives in Minneapolis with her husband. She enjoys walking her dogs, reading, and watching the Minnesota Twins and the Gustavus Adolphus College Men's Soccer Team.